MY TAKE

4

Rafael E. Evangelista

June 2023

Published in USA in June 2023 by
TATAY JOBO ELIZES,
Self-Publisher, under the permission and
authorization of

RAFAEL E. EVANGELISTA
author and copyright owner.

The copyright owner can withdraw this permission
at his discretion without any objection from Tatay
Jobo Elizes at any time. Printing of this book is
using the present day method of Print-On-Demand
(POD) system, where prints will never run out of
copies to be available for posterity.
The copyright owner is free to republish with other
publishers anytime.

KDP ISBN: 9798396518964
Independently Published

Contact: job_elizes@yahoo.com +
https://www.facebook.com/rafael.evangelista.5036459 +
http://tinyurl.com/mj76ccq (amazon site) +
www.tatayjoboelizes.webs.com +
https://www.facebook.com/groups/399368500835109

....

Author

About the author:

Rafael E. Evangelista is a retired capital partner of Baker McKenzie, the largest international law firm in the world.

This is the resume' of Rafael E. Evangelista –

Lawyer, banker, diplomat.
Co-founder, Task Force Good Governance;

Board member, Bank of Commerce (former vice-chairman and executive committee member);

Various memberships in corporate boards

including the Rizal Chapter and the Makati branch of the Philippine National Red Cross;

Board chairman of the NOVA Foundation for the Less Abled;

National Commander, Defenders of Bataan and Corregidor;

and Honorary Consul of the Republic of Lithuania to the the Philippines.

Retired Capital Partner, Baker & Mckenzie (international law practice),
and Member, Board of Trustees, Ateneo de Manila
University.

Attended Ateneo de Manila University (A.B., LI.B.),
Georgetown University (Master of Laws), with an honorary Ph.D. from St. Louis University. Recipient
of the Lithuanian Congressional Gold Medal of Honor.

....

Dedication

Dedication I would like to dedicate this first, and hopefully not last, compendium of essays and poetry written by me to the following:

1. My parents, **Dr. Rafael E Evangelista** and **Encarnacion E. Evangelista**. My father was a real life war hero and a medical doctor who healed at no cost to his patients. In many ways, he was my life's inspiration of "service to others." My mom was the first real writer in

the family. It was she who first encouraged me to write at an early age.

2) My sister, **Rhona E. Centeno**, the other real writer in the family with my mom. She won multiple award for her literary writings. She graduated with two Summa Cum Laude degrees, both completed in four years.

3) **Father Joseph O'Hare S.J.** was my freshman professor in English. He was a pillar of encouragement to my writing. He was the first person who insisted that I publish my works.

4) **Father Miguel Bernad S.J.** was the moderator of the Heights, the literary publication of the Ateneo. He caused the publication of some of my works to encourage me to share my writings with others.

I dedicate this book to these five persons who played such a singular role, each of them, in my literary life. Thank you.

....

Preface and Acknowledgment

Writing has been a passion of mine for almost as long as I can remember. I recall writing essays, short stories and poems as early as the age of 12 years.

Unfortunately, collecting and publishing whatever I had written never warranted the same attention I had given to writing them. Many, if not most of my articles and poems were lost over the years, with little recollection on my part of what, when, and where I wrote. Only a few were ever published.

Most of what I wrote had been scribbled on notebooks and left to fade on forgotten bookshelves. With the advent of computers and cellular phones, my writings were confined to the memory banks of these machines. As the machines turned obsolete, whatever writings were in them were simply confined to oblivion because I never transcribed what I had written.

Obviously, printing and publishing what I had written in the past did not occupy any position of priority in my mind's scheme of things.

I had been writing for many, many years simply for the joy of writing, and the joy of writing was for my self-fulfillment alone. I felt no need to share my thoughts, my dreams, my ambitions with anyone.

Or so I thought!

An old Jesuit professor of mine, Fr. Joseph O'Hare, S.J., who went on to become the President of Fordham University years later, was the first person to jiggle the notion that writing is only half the task of, well, writing! He told my parents at the end of my freshman year at the Ateneo de Manila University that their son was "intellectually selfish." He told them that I had refused to publish anything I had written, even in the school literary digests. The term he actually used to describe me was "intellectual bum."

Fr O'Hare complained to my parents that I had shown no interest in publishing, and hence in sharing, any of my writings. In so many words, he was telling my parents that while I had the talent to write, I was too selfish to share. Fr O'Hare's words did not sink in for many years.

A few years afterwards, another Jesuit professor, Fr. Miguel Bernad S.J., actually had some of my pieces published in the literary magazine of the Ateneo, The Heights, without my knowledge. As before, I had no interest in publishing what I wrote. And Fr. Bernad felt he had to take matters into his own hands.

Giving back was all this fuss was about. My two Jesuit professors and my parents were complicit in reminding me through the years that if someone had been given a gift, the gift was meant to be shared. Writing was only half of my life's mission of writing.

Publishing and sharing with others completed the giving back required.

Although I have self published a number of Haiku poetry books over the past couple of years, this book "My Take 1" is the first comprehensive presentation of my writings - essays and poetry alike. For this effort, I have a new found friend, Jobo Elizes, from across the seas in the United States who encouraged me to publish this book, and beyond that, offered to publish the book himself.

I am grateful to my parents, Fathers O'Hare and Miguel Bernad S.J., and Jobo Elizes for all their encouragement that finally resulted in the publication of this book. I am likewise very grateful to have been afforded the opportunity of giving back and sharing with others, and hope my efforts are worth the reader's while. Rafael E Evangelista 12 May 2023

....

Contents

....

1
Sinagtala Ng Bayani

O mahal na Bayan ko,
Dumating na sa iyong mundo
Ang lubhang sakim ng takipsilim.
Nasaan ang tala sa langit dumilim?

Tayo ay taos pusong lalaban
Na ibalik ang liwanag sa Bayan,

Na ibalik ang Diyos natin banal
Sa Pilipinas nating minamahal.

Nasaan ang duyan ng
Mga magiting na handang
Mamatay para sa iyo, Bayan?
Ibalik ang giting sa ating kabayan!

Lalaban tayo mga anakbayan
Para sa ating sariling kasarinlan;
Ang perlas nating silanganan
Ipagtangol hanggang kamatayan.

Pilipinas aming minumutya.
Pugad ka ng luha at maralita.
Ikaw ay alab ng aming mga puso,
Aming lupain ng bulaklak at ginto.

Pilipinas tayo ay makakalaya na,
Dala ang liwanag ng sinagtala
At simoy ng hanging amihan.
Pag-Asa ng ating Bayan.

Sa manlulupig di tayo pasisiil,
Haharapin natin lahat ng taksil,
Ibabalik ng bayani ang sinagtala
Sa mahal nating Inang Bansa.
(Raffy Evangelista 20 November 2021)

....

2

Maharlika, What's In A Name?

Between the 9th to the 12th Century CE, long
before the Arabs, Chinese, Spaniards, Dutch, British,
Japanese and Americans came to our part of the world,

India was already here in Southeast Asia, including the Philippines. Indian scholars have long referred to the Philippines by the name "Panyupayama" with whom India had a thriving trade and social exchange for a long time.

India divided Southeast Asia into: the Swarnabhumi or Land of Gold, referring to the Mainland of Southeast Asia; the Swanadvipa or Islands of Gold, referring to Maritime Southeast Asia; and Panyupayama or the Land Surrounded by Water, referring to the Philippines. (goo.gl/ok)

Indian culture and language has had profound effects on the Philippines. The word "Datu", for example, is commonly mistaken as Muslim or Arabic. But its origins are in fact derived from Hindu word dhatu - /dhātu/ nf. metal which is of hard substance such as iron or steel. When the Indians arrived in the Philippines and Southeast Asia, they introduced metals to the early island settlers. Since metals before were a rare find, the Indians, and later every person who possessed or owned metals, were considered to have high status in society, and were called "datus."

What is my point in discussing India's influence on the Philippines? It has to do with the name of our country, the "Philippines," and the desire of some to change that name to what they say is the "Muslim/Arabic based word Maharlika." (They claim the word "Maharlika" is Muslim/Arabic in origin. In fact, "Maharlika" actually traces its roots to India). And the stated justification of the proponents of the change? Maharlika was the original name of the Philippines, or so the proponents assert.

This suggestion to rename the Philippines to Maharlika has been around for some time. In fact, two Philippine Presidents, despite being separated by roughly 45 years, have tried to "reinstall" the "old" name of the country, "Maharlika."

President Ferdinand Marcos is credited with the first attempt to change the country's name from "Philippines" to "Maharlika." The ostensible reason given by Marcos for his suggested change of name was that the "Philippines" was a name foisted on us by our colonial masters of the time, Spain, whereas the name "Maharlika" was the country's original name given by early Arab and Muslim settlers.

As fate would have it, Marcos had a duplicitous motive for his suggested change of country name. Marcos' nom de guerre during WW II, by his own claim, was "Maharlika." Marcos' suggested change of name was a blatant attempt to name the country after himself.

Roughly 45 years later, President Duterte, again floated the idea of renaming the Philippines to Maharlika. The reason given was so that this country would revert back to its original historical name, Maharlika, and not bear the name Filipinas, a name identified with the King Felipe of Spain.

But one wonders if Duterte, like Marcos, had a hidden motive in wanting to change the country's name from Philippines to Maharlika. Remember it was Duterte who has slavishly heaped praise on Marcos as a great leader, despite the evidence that the latter was a despot who ruled the country for 20 years, mostly under Martial Law, stole billions of dollars from the public coffers, imprisoned his political enemies or worse.

And it was Duterte who had Marcos buried in the Libingan Ng Mga Bayani despite the public condemnation of such a move. Could Duterte, have been really playing to the dying wish, so to speak, of Marcos to name the country Maharlika after himself? What greater honor could Duterte pay to his beloved predecessor beyond burying Marcos as a national hero in the Libingan Ng Mga Bayani? Simple! Rename the whole country in the name of Marcos, aka Maharlika!

But historical precedent for the name change to Maharlika simply isn't there. The pretext given for the change is that "Maharlika" is the original name of the Philippines. That claim is historically wrong. The oldest known name that the Philippines was known by was the Hindu or Indian name "Panyupayama." There is simply no historical "first name" basis for renaming the Philippines to "Maharlika." On a "primo geniture" basis, Panyupayama has first rights to claim that honor!

Personally, I am in favor of the retention of the name "Philippines." So much of our history and culture is focused on that name. Besides, "Filipinos" has a nice ring to it. I am not sure I can say the same thing about "Panyupayamans" or in a shortened form "Payamans!" "Payamans"has such a vile connotation to it! It reminds me too much of those who tried to author the change of name! (Rafael E Evangelista, 14 April 2021)

....

3
*Excerpts from the Wikipedia article on Bongbong Marcos

(*How can a man who has never known hardship, who never carried a cross, know what it is to be poor? presume to lead a people who are 80% poor? Following is a narration of documented statements.)

Bongbong Marcos was born on September 13, 1957. He was 8 years old when his father was elected President in 1965. And thus, Malacañang was his family's place of residence for 20 years, until they were booted out in 1986. BBM was 28 when they left Malacañang.

Education

He was 13 in 1970, when he "was sent to England where he lived and studied at the Worth School, an all-boys Benedictine institution." "He then enrolled at St Edmund Hall, Oxford to read Politics, Philosophy, and Economics (PPE). However, despite his false claims that he graduated with a BA in Philosophy, Politics and Economics,[20] he did not obtain a degree.[21] "Marcos enrolled in the Masters in Business Administration program at the Wharton School of Business, University of Pennsylvania in Philadelphia, U.S., which he failed to complete. In a statement, he claimed he withdrew from the program for his election as Vice Governor of Ilocos Norte in 1980. "In the book Some Are Smarter than Others, author Ricardo Manapat reveals that after the EDSA revolution, investigators of the Presidential Commission on Good Government found out that the Marcos Jr' tuition, USD 10,000 monthly allowance, and the estate he lived in while studying at Wharton were paid using funds that could be traced partly to the intelligence funds of the Office of the President, and partly to some of the 15 bank accounts that the Marcoses had secretly opened in the US under assumed names.[26]

Early Political Life

After 10 years spent mostly abroad, BBM returned to the Philippines in 1980, at the age of 23, to become Vice Governor of Ilocos Norte. He then replaced his aunt Elizabeth Keon as Governor in 1983 and served until 1986 when they were booted out of Malacañang. He was not an innocent boy, but instead was already Governor of Ilocos Norte when they left Malacañang. It was during this early political period when BBM did not file nor pay income tax returns. "In 1995, the Quezon City Regional Trial Court Judge Benedicto Ulep convicted Marcos to seven years in jail and a fine of US$2,812 plus back taxes for tax evasion in his failure to file an income tax return from the period of 1982 to 1985 while sitting as the Governor of Ilocos Norte.[66]"

"During the last days of the 1986 People Power Revolution, Bongbong Marcos, in combat fatigues to project his warlike stance,[41] pushed his father Ferdinand Marcos to give the order to his remaining troops attack and blow up Camp Crame despite the presence of hundreds of thousands of civilians there, nevertheless, the elder Marcos did not follow his son's urgings.[42]" (*Footnote 42 Lustre Jr., Philip (February 25, 2016). "Ferdinand Marcos: His last day at the Palace". CNN Philippines).

Later Political Life

"Bongbong Marcos was among the first of the Marcos family to return to the Philippines in 1991, and soon sought political office, beginning in the family's traditional bailiwick in Ilocos Norte.[50]"

He was elected Congressman of the 2nd District of Ilocos Norte and served from 1992 to 1995. "In 1995, Marcos ran for a seat in the Philippine Senate but lost.[56]" "BBM was elected Governor of Ilocos Norte in 1998" and served until 2007 after being reelected two more times.

In 2007, no longer eligible to run as Governor, he ran and was elected Congressman again. In 2010 he ran as Senator, winning this time, and served until 2016. In 2016 he ran for Vice-President, and lost to Leni Robredo.

Personal Life

"Marcos Jr is married to Louise "Liza" Cacho Araneta, with three sons: Ferdinand Alexander III "Sandro" (born 1994), Joseph Simon (born 1995) and William Vincent "Vince" (born 1997).[132][133][additional citation(s) needed] Although some attribute him as Ilocano, he does not know how to speak the Ilocano language.[134]"

(Collated by Raffy Evangelista, 2021)

4
Red or Black

The SOD (son of the dictator) has chosen the color Red as his campaign color. Red was the color of the blood of martyrs who died during martial rule! Red is the color of blood shed during the EJKs by this administration. Let the people remember what the campaign color chosen by this SOD really represents- the blood of our fellow Filipinos killed during two eras of the greatest injustice committed by two so called leaders that he, the SOD, is closely identified with. By using red, the SOD mocks and insults our heroic dead. Note that his choice of Red was announced ironically on All Souls Day!

My father and his companions served in WW II, where many of them lost their lives, shed their blood or were severely injured. The blood they shed for our country was courageous Red. It is such an insult for the SOD to choose the same color when his father had to fake his military exploits in order to be awarded war medals he never earned. It is atrocious that the SOD would choose the color of courage, when his grandfather was executed for treachery to the Philippines during the War.

The SOD does not deserve to use the color Red for his campaign to win the hearts and minds of Filipinos. Black is the only color that he and his family and close political cohorts deserve to use. Black is the color of their hearts!

Raffy Evangelista November 2, 2021

5
Lux In Domino

Each one of us is a star.
Even if sometimes, nights
Take our shine away;
Even if clouds and rain
Try to drown our light.

Sometimes we shine
With the rest; and
Sometimes we twinkle alone.
Shine and realize
That we may be the only
Light for someone
In times of darkness.

Be the light that
Can only see good...
Be the light that forgives
The worst...
Be the light that forgets
The bad...
Be the light that fights
Evil...
Be the light in the Lord!

As we journey
in these uncertain times
groping our way,
Be the light of our faith.
Let our light of
Hope and love
Help others see
Life through.

Let our light be
The Lux in Domino
That will shine
On others.
Let our light be
The Light of the Lord!

(REE, 2020)

....

6
Weaponizing Politics In Religion

I am totally incredulous how even politics has been weaponized by some of our Christian religious denominations. We have been told is so many words that the world will be damned or at least severely punished if we do not vote or support this or that politician. And that we must believe their prophets because they are true spokesmen of Christ, even if we do not belong to the denomination or denominations of these propagandists. I do not believe God will condemn us for not believing the words of these self anointed prophets, who we sincerely believe are ordinary men.

As I intimated before, followers of Pastor Quiboloy may swear to high heavens that Quiboloy is both a prophet and the Second Coming of Christ himself. But, I am sorry, when Quiboloy endorsed Dutit as the rightful President of our country, I had enough proof that Quiboloy is a fake prophet, and certainly not The Christ! And when certain Christian prophets endorse Dutit with his innumerable sins, faults, shortcomings, warts and all, as the rightful leader of the Free World, I started wondering if these prophets are divinely inspired or not.

But this is based on my less than 20/20 vision and insights alone. My Christian friends from other denominations are entitled in the exercise of their free will and best judgement to disagree with me on Dutit. BUT with one major caveat, I will never insist that they are damned for not agreeing with me!

Which brings me back to my original thesis: All Christians of all denominations should work together for the salvation of all mankind on the basis of our one common and unifying factor, our belief in Jesus Christ. Carping on the differences between us, eg: that praying for Mary's intercession is idolatry, can only be counterproductive and divisive. You tell me that Mary represents idolatrous worship, and I for one will dig my heels in for I know it isn't so. You tell me that Jesus is our true God and the 2nd Person of the Trinity, I will go forward with you hand in hand, all the way.

I truly believe our Lord gives much more weight to our honoring Him together as one family, rather than wasting our precious time honoring and applauding our differences.

And So We Should Proclaim, Together As One, "All For The Greater Glory of God! Ad Majorem Dei Gloriam!"

(Raffy Evangelista, 27 December 2021)

....

7
Francis Burton Harrison

Governor-General Francis Burton Harrison, a towering political figure against anti-imperialism in the Philippines. He died a Philippine Citizen. Not too many Filipinos know much about him. –

On October 6, 1913, Francis Burton Harrison, beloved by the Filipinos, assumed office as the 6th Governor-General of the U.S. Insular Government of the Philippines. His appointment to the office, though, was dated September 2, 1913. His term lasted until 1921.

Given his anti-imperialist stand, Harrison was appointed by U.S. President Woodrow Wilson to ameliorate the U.S. governance of the Philippines. As Governor-General, Harrison sought independence for the Philippines and introduced reforms that placed more Filipinos in administrative positions, which prepared them for self-government.

Harrison returned to the Philippines in 1935 to serve as an adviser to President Manuel Quezon. A year later, he expressed to Quezon his desire to become a Filipino citizen. Quezon immediately wrote a letter about this to Hon. Gil Montilla, then-Speaker of the National Assembly. Weeks later, the National Assembly passed Commonwealth Act No. 79, which conferred Filipino citizenship on Harrison.

During World War II, Harrison also served the Philippine government-in-exile in Washington, D.C. He again served as a special adviser to the Presidents Manuel Roxas, Elpidio Quirino, and Ramon Magsaysay.

Harrison died on November 21, 1957 at Hunterdon Medical Center in New Jersey. He willed that he be buried in the Philippines so his body was shipped from the U.S. He was given a state funeral and was buried in the Manila North Cemetery.

Harrison Park in Manila and F. B. Harrison Avenue in Pasay were named in Harrison's honor.

(REE, 2021)

....

8

Catholics and Evangelicals, Brothers or Foes? Oneness in Christ

It is always tragic when otherwise good Christians weaponize natural epidemics and disasters to further their religious biases at the expense of fellow Christians.

I recently heard an Evangelical friend for whom I have the greatest respect, use the COVID pandemic, perhaps inadvertently, as a political tool to speak against Catholicism and Catholics. In a conference, he pointed out among others that the devotion of Italians to Mary has only resulted in a great many COVID cases in Catholic Italy.

I couldn't help but reflect on what he said. By the same token, I thought, what does that say about largely Protestant and Evangelical United States which has currently the highest incidence of the virus in the world? On the other hand, what does that say about Vietnam which is Communist, and yet has a very low incidence of contamination?

An avid Catholic, another good friend of mine, sometimes makes sly allusions against Protestant Christians on behalf of conservative Catholicism. Which makes me cringe because he sometimes chooses to say those things, when non Catholic Christians are present. I have heard him say gratuitously out of the blue without any real need to pontificate that only Catholics trace their origins directly to Christ, implying perhaps that Jesus will respond only to the prayers of Catholics during this pandemic.

Yes, Christians of all stripes are, sometimes, guilty of weaponizing religion. And I wonder whether one of the lessons our Lord wants all of us to learn from this pandemic is that we must do battle as one, that that mankind is far too divided, nation against nation, people against people, faiths against faiths.

Rather than emphasizing differences between various Christian denominations specially during this severely divisive and trying times of the pandemic, shouldn't all Christians, in fact all Filipinos regardless of creed, be trying hard to come together to wage battle as one people? For Christians, shouldn't they be addressing this pandemic on the basis of their unifying factor, Christ, and battle the virus together as brothers of and in the Faith, regardless of their religious differences?

Ironically, the same Christians of all denominations who would weaponize religion, are the first to fall in line beneath the banner and the slogan of unity and solidarity: "We will overcome the pandemic together as one." I wonder if they all understand that "One" means all Filipinos, marching hand in hand together, regardless of religious beliefs.

Catholic Christians and Evangelical Christians should never be the enemies of one another, specially during this pandemic, and beyond. The common enemy now is the virus and Satan, not each other.

Sloganeering will not work unless we live and give life to our words. Let us all be One in Christ!

(REE, 3 May 2020)

....

9

MMDA Regulation 2020

This is an active and true account of what happened to me today –

Today, Friday, Jan 5, 2021, I had to have prostate treatment at Veterans Memorial Hospital in Quezon City. My treatment started about 11:00 am and finished about 11:45am.

By the time I left the hospital, it was past 12nn. I decided to stop at a nearby mall, Eton Centris Mall, which has a restaurant, Ramen Kuroda, to have lunch.

For reference purposes, my home (in Muntinlupa) is about 30 km away. Perhaps a one and a half hour drive, depending on the traffic.

When I got to the restaurant, I was told they couldn't service me because of my age. They pointed out that this was pursuant to a MMDA Regulation (Regulation 2020 - 03, Series of 2020) and local ordinance which prohibits those of 65 years and above from stepping out of their homes.

I am 80 years old. I had to go Veterans Memorial Hospital at 11 am for prostate treatment. At 2pm today, I was supposed to go to the Lung Center for radiation treatment. There simply was no way for me to run home for lunch before my treatment at the Lung Center.

Why is all this relevant? The MMDA Circular and implementing city ordinance has deprived me from securing food between my two medical protocols today. Think about the implications: the MMDA Regulation prevented me from securing food! Sustenance can be critical to persons with medical conditions !

If I am now being told I have no right to food, who knows whether citizens, 65 and over, like me, may one day be told they cannot go to hospitals to secure medical treatment. After all, the MMDA Regulation and implementing ordinance make no distinction on the purpose of stepping outside the home. 65 years and above, full stop, the prohibition applies. And the prohibition is absolute!

Ridiculous and absurd as it may seem, it can happen!

This is an example of the brainless and thoughtless mindset of Government favoring the strong arm tactic of lockdowns, without consideration of the implication of the Constitutional Right of all that no one, including seniors above 65, can be "deprived of liberty without due process." (Sec I, Article 3, Bill of Rights, Philippine Constitution)

(REE, 5 January 2021)

....

10
WE ARE ONE

Black lives matter!
But why do we have
To be reminded
That this is so?
Black, white, yellow, brown,
All lives matter!
All children, all one people,
under one God!
Color, does it really matter?
Why judge others
On the basis of color?
It is people who matter:
Their hearts, their minds,
Their souls!

White is really pink,
And black Is really
A shade of brown,
And yellow and brown
Are shades in between!
We are all people of color!
Black lives matter,
Of course they do,

As all lives do!
Fight for all discriminated
Against because of color!
Color "cattle" brands
One race from another,
One race against the other.
Color branding says
"Stop, you are white!"
"Stop, you are black!"

Stop telling people
Of a different shade
To return to where
They come from!
We are all one people,
From God in one world!
That is where
We All belong!
That is what
We all call "Home!"
All lives matter,
We all do!
Color really doesn't!

(REE, 2 June 2020)

....

11
A Call For Change In Mindset

Filipinos must start condemning the "petty, personal attacks" that have become rife in Philippine politics. They must call on government officials, starting with President Duterte, to follow the examples of our great Filipino Statesmen of yesteryears who raised and debated issues, rather than personalities: Presidents Quezon, Osmena, Senators Recto and Diokno, among others.

The season of divisiveness in the country has become so deep that it is critical that we reject what has become far too common in our country: name calling, petty personal attacks, doing and saying whatever it takes just stay in power or to get one's way in politics.

It is dangerous to continue to do so, specially when we are exposed not just internal, but more specially to external threats, the likes of which the Philippines has not seen since Imperial Japan tried to impose on Southeast Asia it's much proclaimed "Japanese Co-Prosperity Sphere." The Belt-Road program of China and its 9 Yard Dash Line in the South China Sea clearly proclaims China's intention to take over Southeast Asia and beyond, darkly echoing what Imperial Japan tried to do 80 years ago.

To continue to be so divided as a people not only lessens who we are as a country, but also stops us from recognizing fully as one nation the kind of threat China poses for the Philippines today.

There must be a better way forward. We can work with people who are different from us. We can be friends with people who are different from us. We can love and care about people who are different than us. We can keep people who are different than us safe. We can be good people who care deeply about each other even when we disagree.

We can start by listening to someone with a different opinion—listening not to rebut or debate, but listening to understand. We can articulate our own opinions and beliefs without believing or saying that someone else's are, therefore, wrong. We can embrace difference while seeking common ground.

Trolling one another, fighting one another on social media or any other kind of media is simply not the answer.

We must all agree to "double down" on such an inclusive approach, vowing to represent the Filipino people "not by calling names or playing political games, but by showing up and doing the work to keep Philippines moving forward."

We must all reflect on the legacy left behind by our hero statesmen who dedicated their lives for a united and greater Philippines, among them our martyrs Josefa Llanes Escoda, Jose Abad Santos and Vicente Lim. They sacrificed their lives for all Filipinos. Trolling and fighting one another diminishes Filipinos as a people and the Philippines as a country.

Unity may be the only way we can survive the double whammy of external and internal threats like China and Typhoon Odette. I am not suggesting that we agree to crimes and wrong doing. People should be called to task for that. But in the very least, we can agree to disagree, and at the end of the day still remain one people and one country by simply not being disagreeable.

(REE, 20 December 2021)

....

12
Haiku Compilation:

Comedy

You must keep laughing.
Life is just a comedy
Between tears and fears.

Stand

I stand with my God
I will not falter for He
Also stands by me.

Dogs

Dogs are expensive.
Not for money, but for love.
Love cannot be bought.

Beyond Grief
Trying to see beyond,
I try to smile through my grief,
Not sure what to do.

Songs

The glorious sunrise
Stirs a cacophony of
Songs from forest tops.

Board Room

What's the diff –
Board room
And bored room
where talk and talk
Go nowhere quickly?

The Real Fool

How often have I judged
Some other to be a fool,
To find I am him?

Different Journeys

There is a journey
That everyone undertakes,
Different for each one.

Sunshine

Life is a journey:
Beyond the cold mountains and
Dark valleys, sunshine!

What Choice?

Swim against the tide
Or be swept out to the sea.
Do we have a choice?

Kisses On The Sand

Have you heard the song
Of waves kissing nearby shores?
Music strumming sand!

Grace

Grace transforms the land.
Behold!
Once barren deserts
Bear verdant flowers.

Taste Of Heaven

God meant for us to
Have a taste of heaven
With every sunrise.

Reminders

Have you ever thought:
Our furry pets are gifts to
Remind us of love?

The Coming

Be still for I am wind!
Be still for I am earthquake'
We proclaim He comes!

Thank You

Thank You, Lord, thank You.
For the beauty around us.
Thank You for Your love.

All Hands

One hand cannot clap.
Unity must come to all
For a people to stand.

Take The Risk

Journeys you will take
Can change your life forever.
Climb! Risk the mountain!

Empty Chair

The wicker chair stands

Empty, waiting.
My father Used to sit on it.

Memories

I think memories,
Whether they're happy or sad,
Define who I am.

Circus

Home is your castle,
But do not create a circus
By sending in clowns.

Save The Forests

Look to the towering trees
Majestic in verdant green!
Yet man cuts them down!

Heroes

We need more heroes.
Even trees need solid roots
To withstand the winds.

Spring

Spring isn't just greens…
Flower rainbows in meadows,
Sunlight's glow in streams.

What Have I Done

I ask you again.
What have I ever done for
You to turn away?

Daughter

*It matters not if
Your blood does not run In mine.
You are my daughter.*

Jesus

Jesus,

*You are God,
My Redeemer and My King.
There is none like You!*

Lisp

*A friend laughed at my
Funny accent.
He did not Know about my lisp.*

Incoherent

*Though thoughts do not flow,
Sometimes, the words can rumble
On, and on, and on.*

Imaginary Playmates

*One is never too old
To run and play in playgrounds
With good friends long gone.*

Acceptance

*No malice, just smiles.
The baby coos at strangers
Who tickle her toes.*

(Raf Evangelista, 28 February 2023)

Dead End?

The sign reads one way.
Sometimes this sign really means
Dead end at the end.

Way Out?

Is there a way out?
The forests are deep with dark
Promises to keep!

Co-Pilot

Life is a journey.
God is our co-pilot.
He will guide the way.

Stop And Look

Stop, look, and listen!
Even along lighted paths
One can still stumble.

Hold On

Hold on to my hand.
We travel towards the light
Beyond dark mountains.

Feel

Have you felt the warmth
Shine from love and happiness?
It is here! Feel it!

Aim For The Stars

I promise you, Love,
Dead ends will not hinder us
From grasping the stars!

Nightfall Meditation

As the shadows fall,
Clouds drift about the mountain sides,
Searching for the moon.

Haunting Song

Sea waves lap unseen
In the setting dusk of night,
Singing their haunting song.

Good night Call

A solitary
Bird calls out to the stars
To bid them good night.

Golden Scepter

I call to my God
That the sun will once more raise
His Golden Scepter!

Colors

Crimson and gold hues
Reach to dark purple heavens,
Seeking gold of stars.

Interface

*Interface with God
In pink blossoms of the fields,
And golden sunrise.*

Touch

*Feel His gentle touch
In the soft breezes that blow
In the springtime morn.*

Noonday Dance

*In the brillance of
God's noonday sun, look to trees
That dance in the wind.*

Starry Fireflies

*Then as the sun sets
Watch His stars spread their magic
Of fireflies above.*

Bask

*Bask in His splendor
In the soft glow of the moon
In the purple sky.*

Warming

*And as night deepens,
Look to His warming embrace
In night's solitude.*

Feel God

Interface with God.

Feel Him in all creation
And all its splendor.

Everywhere

Be at peace, be loved.
God is all around in light
And even darkness.

What Future?

Fight for the future
By remembering the past,
Both the good and bad.

Past, Present, Future

There is no future
If we ignore the present,
Which comes from the past.

Today

Plant the seeds today
So children can see the trees
And the flowers bloom.

Barren

Look at the barren
Mountain tops stripped of cover,
And think of the young.

Desolation

Stark desolation,
This is the world we may leave
To our children.

Build

Do build if we must.
But not by destroying hope
For a verdant world.

The Eyes Of The Child

Look into the eyes
Of a child.
What do you see? For now, hopelessness!

Verdant

His world could be filled
With carpets of bright flowers
On verdant meadows.

Faith, Hope, Gratitude

And with faith and hope,
We could leave him with a world
Where he can thank God!
The Brave (A Tribute To Leila De Lima)

I Will Not Cower
I will not cower
Even if they silence me
And take my freedoms.

Seeing God

I have not seen light
In the six years they kept me,
But I have seen God.

For God, For Country

*There is a time for
All men to make this judgment:
For God, for Country!*

True Heroes

*Only brave heroes
Know the bright meaning of love,
Overcoming fear.*

Onward For Others

*I fight for others,
And not just for my beliefs.
God guides me onward!*

Vindication

*Vindication comes!
It will come one day, and soon:
I fight for the just!*

Haikus on Love:

*In A Mother's Touch
What can ever match
A mother's loving embrace?
God is in her touch.*

Love Is About

*The love of a child
Now gone when parents are old.
What ever happened?*

True Love

*True love is known when
There is no benefit to
Gained in giving.*

You Are Called

*Do those who are poor
Have friends to support and
Love them? You are called!*

Put Away The Cellphones

*They may not ask, but
Family need your attention.
Put away the cellphones!*

Saying Goodbye

*Those who loved you best
Need you beside them when they
Are saying, "Goodbye!"*

No Expectations

*If you love others,
Have no expectations that
They can never meet.*

The Approaching Day
(The Tribulation)

The Way

*Faith is not for sale!
Fight tall, fight strong, and fight free!
God will make a way!*

God's Armor

*Dark winds of war blow
Both here and abroad the land.
We seek God's armor!*

We Seek You

*Where can we find You, Lord?
In the great Tribulation,
Let us not despair!*

Written

*The craven seek
Man's Downfall, but it is written
That God will prevail.*

Your People

*We believe in Your Love.
You, O Lord, will conquer all.
We are your people.*

Great Shaking

*Focus all our love
On Christ. In the great shaking,
He will come to save!*

Haikus On Life

Go

*My father led me
To the forest edge,
And said, "Go your way!"*

Where Do I go?

"But there are no tracks,"
I said. "Where am I to go?"
As he bade me goodbye.

Farewell

The mist covered him
As he disappeared in the
Setting of the sun.

Life's Beginning

My own life began when
I trudged down forest trails
As stars led my way.

Discovery of Self

I found myself when
My father let me go on
Into the unknown.

Flying

His was the wisdom
Of the ages that allowed
Me to fly to the skies.

Curtain Call

The vast night sky turns
Peach, tangerine, violet
At day's curtain call.

Curtsy Dance

Stars blink and curtsy

From constellations sailing
In the high heavens.

Pantomine

A misty dawn breaks
In pantomine play at dusk,
Tickling grey mountains.

Ripples

The soft mist ripples
Over tree tops shimmering
In the morning breeze.

Gold Throne

The clouds dissipate.
The orb reigns from its gold throne,
Among dark blue skies.

Sun God

Slowly descending,
The sun god presides over
Seas of burnished gold.

Vermillion

Streaks of vermillion
Across the cobalt heavens,
Paint rippling waves.

The Moon

The luminous moon glows
Brightly as the sun fades in
The indigo back drop.

The Tears Are Gone

*God painted my heart
With colors of happiness.
I can't hide my smile.*

Specks?

*What are we- you, I ?
Specks in the Cosmos of God,
Clinging to His Hand!*

The Truth?

*You alter the facts
To fit what you believe in!
Where then is God's truth?*

Renewal

*True love does not stop
Just because of the sunset.
Sunrise brings new life!*

Be Worthy

*Be worthy of love,
Be in love for a lifetime.
Any less is a waste.*

Guiding Hand

*In the rush of day,
Fall back on love and believe.
A Hand guides the way.*

Morning Kiss

*The sun rises
And kisses flowers sleeping
On pillows of mist.*

Night Dance

*The orange curtain
Falls, and shadows orchestrate
A strange dance of night.*

Two Stars

*Two lights whirl up high
In the night sky - a firefly*

Waltzing with a star.

Sky Diamonds

*I search the dark sky,
And in the night, diamonds
Embrace me softly.*

Sky Painting

*The fires of heaven
Toss crimson across the skies,
Burnt gold on canvass.*

Chase

*Chasing the rainbow,
I follow the drifting raindrops,
And wait for the sun.*

Listen

Nothing to something...
Listen to the darkness, and
Hear the angels sing.

Forgiveness

He wrote all our sins
On drifting sands, and etched
His Love on solid rock.

Embers

In the despair of
Darkest winter burns softy
Salvific embers.

Distant Light

A faint light flickers.
A star or a newborn babe?
I fall on my knees!

(Raf Evangelista, Compiled: 1 March 2023)

....

13
A poem for pet lovers-

BEFORE THE BRIDGE

Dear Mama:

Is it, as the old song goes,
"Time now to say goodbye?"
Well, only God truly knows
When pets do cross the sky.

I know that day will come.
It is the "when" I cannot say.
God chooses for all, not some,
Even as you kneel and pray.

Mama, should I say goodbye?
Perhaps soon, and maybe today.
But even as the light might die,
It is only God who can truly say.
So rather than say goodbye,
Please pray today for me
That in God's towering sky
His Face I will shortly see.
Parting does not mean forever.
We are meant to meet again.
We are meant to be together
At the distant rainbow's end.
Weep not for me for when I go
To beyond that far off bend,
I shall forever love you so…
Mama,I truly love you so!
Your Golden Retriever, Chelsea

(Raf Evangelista, 13 March , 2023)

....

14
A Proposal

Darling: I kneel before you,
And this is what I ask of you:

No matter where we go,
No matter what we do,
Please be there for me,
As I will always be there for you.

Say you need me with you,
Here beside you.
Anywhere you go, let me go too.
That's all I ask of you.
Say you'll share with me
One love, one lifetime;
Say the word and I will follow you.
Share each day with me,
Each night, each morning.
Say you love me!
That's what I ask of you!

And if you answer "yes,"
There's one more thing for you to do:
I am gettng old.
May I be so bold
As to ask of you
To be true –
Help me up off my knees.
They are also in their eighties.

(REE, 26 May 2030, with due apologies to the author of Phantom of the Opera)

....

15
I Walked Into Your Life

I walked into your life
When I was lost and hurting.
When I fell in love with you,
You were taking a chance
By letting me walk into your life,
And letting me love you.
You knew where I'd been,
About my past, and were

*Willing to give me the chance
To fall in love again.
You never asked even if
You had the right to do so.
I walked into your life
When I was lost, and then
I fell in love with you.
I never thought I would
Find anybody else.
It had been so long.
But then I fell in love again
When you softly smiled,
And very gently said, "hello."
I walked into your life.
You took a chance with me.
When I was searching.
You gave me the chance
To fall in love once again,
To fall in love … with you.
I will never let you go.
I fell in love with you when
I was lost and hurting.
I walked into your life,
And I fell in love with you!
And now years after,
I still do! I really do!*

REE, 22 June 2022)

....

16
WE ARE SPINNING

(In the maelstrom of bad politics)

*Our country is spinning
In tyrannical cycles.
This island home we're in
Turns in dangerous circles.*

*Day in, day out,
Where are we going?
Beyond the turnabouts,
Dark winds are blowing.*

*Turning and turning,
Blowing to a spinning spin.
We are stumbling, fleeing,
In and out, and out and in.*

*No longer any rhyme or
Reason to frenetic turns,
Unmindful of scraping, falling
And those painful burns.*

*Dizzying, dizzying, dizzying.
How, where, and when to go?
Here to there, to anywhere,
The scalawags blunder so!*

*To some, the evil is not real.
If so, what then is false or true?
Who then is to ask: who lies?
Is it me, or the devil in you?*

*A lie? A farce? The circle
Turns, and truth to tell,
The evil one still reigns,
And he was born in hell.*

Perhaps to flow and to slide

With the changing tides is best.
But will we live through, survive
This lonely, desperate test?

Our people are embattled.
But fight We must, fight to live, eat, sleep.
For foreboding darkness gathers
In the circling, treacherous deep.

The world is spinning
Bewilderingly, frightfully so.
We need to fight, to hold on,
Till evil is finally let go.

(Raf Evangelista 16 December 2021)

....

17
Zarzuela

The elaborate zarzuela being foisted on us by the Duterte father and daughter and their acolytes would be amusing if not for the fact that the joke is on us Filipinos. They shamelessly peddle the lie that they seek office not for their own gain but to serve the people and complete unfinished business.

You dread what they mean by that. After all they presided over a country that has performed the worst in responding to the pandemic, that has plunged precipitously down the global corruption index, and reversed decades of economic growth to yet again become ' the sick man of Asia'.

Where Pharmally and Udena will forever become the epitome of cronyism unmatched in our history. Where they have set the record for killing its own people through its murderous anti-drug war, EJKs, and its botched handling of the pandemic. Where instead of fighting for our sovereignty it has willingly subverted it to a foreign regime in exchange for unfulfilled promises of economic largesse for the country.

Rodrigo, the father, in a fit of pique over his petulant daughter, has put forward his bag carrier, the "pambansang photobomber" to be the next President of our beleaguered country to perpetuate his misrule. His confidence stems from his being able to get his court jesters elected to the Senate. Thus inspired, Panelo and Roque, have thrown their jester hats into the (circus) ring . And just so he got all bases covered, their master has also joined the fun.

Sara, the daughter and reigning denial queen, has teamed up with the feckless son of our only other despot to date. The son who relies entirely on his surname since he has little to show in terms of accomplishment for his entire public life and who even lied about his education.

Which is why he employs an army of trolls to burnish his name by changing the narrative about his father being a hero rather than the plunderer that destroyed our economy and who was responsible for the death and disappearance of thousands of our countrymen.

He tells us to move on while he files a claim for the rest of the plundered wealth that is not yet in his family's hands. But he has more than enough means to revise history, delude our people and defame the opposition with his vast army of trolls. Means stolen from us. "Niluluto tayo sa ating sariling mantika."

Would it not be to our eternal shame as a people, admired by the world for our courage to peacefully overthrow the failed Marcos regime, only to elect the unrepentant son who is a convicted tax cheater to boot?

Do we really want more of these kind of leaders in the next six years or more? Enough is enough. We have been made fools enough by these self- proclaimed saviors. Let us stop this cycle of electing politicians so they can enrich themselves while impoverishing the rest of our people with their misgovernance and corruption.

We should by right feel angry, aggrieved and abused. Let us regain the moral compass that we have somehow lost along the way. Let us put faith in strength of character, competence, honesty, decency, and empathy for the common good.

(2002)

....

18
Ako Ang Bagyo

They cackled, "Kaya mo
Ba ang darating na bagyo?"
She whispered:
"Ako ang bagyo.
Tayo'y di magpapaloko!"

Cool winds sing and whisper,
As Leni gathers the rain showers.
So watch and marvel: good, not
Evil, will be arriving soon after.

There are good storms after all,
All who thirst will come to realize.
To the dry, starving fields below,
Leni in time will comes to fertilize.

The future goodness of Leni's rain
Will bring singing to dry streams,
Green cover to leafless trees,
Drizzles to subdued sunbeams.

*Rainbows will cross our land
And birds will sing and fly
Freely among rain showers
Sent down from God's sky.*

*Be ready for Leni.
She is the brewing storm
That brings the rainbows.
She is the coming norm.*

*"Ako ang bagyo na padating.
Dala ko ang hanging amihan.
Huwag matakot at magatubili.
I am a good storm, kabayan."*

Ako si Leni!

(Raffy Evangelista, 10 November 2021)

....

19
Hidden Message

A loving friend recently told me that she is so thankful to the Lord for granting everything she asked for in a life partner. I was so happy to hear that what she prayed for had been granted. Then she told me that she had told God that I need not be good looking. I am still wondering if there was the hidden message in her statement!

(REE, 20 April 2030)

....

20
Kaibigan:

Alam ko kaalyado mo si Du30 at pamilya ni FM, ang dating diktador. Kaya pinadalan mo ako ng anti Leni video.

Meron akong gustong itanong sa iyo.

Ilang beses nagsinungaling si Du30 sa Bayan? Ilan beses siya nagpalit ng isip? Ilan beses siya biglang kumambyo at nagsabi na sya ay nagbibiro. Ilang libong Pilipino ang pinatay na walang hustisya o trial? Ilan maid at babae ang minolest nya? Ilan katao ang namatay dahil sa sama ng pandemic response nya? Pinagmumura nya ang Santo Papa and inutos nyang papatayin ang mga Obismo. Bagsak ang ekonomia.

Ganoon din, Ilan beses nagsinunaling ang diktador si FM sa taon bayan? Ninakawan pa tayo ng bilyon bilyon dolyar at nagpatay ng libo libo din sa ilalalim ng Martial Law.

Si Imelda na convict na abroad at dito sa pagnanakaw ng bilyon bilyon dolyar, lahat pera ng Bayan. Bagsak din ang ekonomia noong Presidente ang asawa nya.

At yung anak ng dictator si FM, na nakinabang sa nakaw, wala daw syang alam, wala syang kasalanan. Ano ang katotohanan tungkol sa anak ng diktador? Palso ang diploma nya sa Oxford - Hindi degree diploma ang natanggap nya. Nakatira sya sa mansion at mga Rolls Royce na sasakyan habang nasa England.

Bago yung EDSA Revolution, sya ay meron katungkulan na opisyal sa Probinsya ng Ilocos. Ngayon sinasabi nya wala syang alam sa pagnanakaw nila?

Meron final and executory judgement(s) na ang Swiss Courts contra sa Marcos na kailangan ibalik sa Bayan ang bilyon bilyon na ninakaw nila. Kung walang ninakaw nila sa Bayan, bakit pinapabalik ng Swiss Court ang pera sa Bayan?

Hindi daw alam ng anak ng diktador?

Pwede bang hindi alam nitong anak ng diktador ang desisyon ng Swiss Courts? Pero walang paghingi man ng paumanhin. Walang offer na ibalik yung naiiwan nakaw yaman na di pa nababalik.

Yan ba ay isang leader totoo sa Bayan? Para alam mo, ako personal ay biktima ng Martial Law ng Diktador. Hindi man ako pinatay, kinulong o tinorture, biktima pa rin. Ni raid at hinalungkat ang buong bahay ko noong eary days ng Martial Law. Subversive daw ako. Wala naman silang nakita sa bahay.

Ganoon pa man, nag impose sila ng travel ban sa akin na umabot ng 6 years. Pakatapos na lang na EDSA Revolt ako naka byahe ulit. Sa trabaho ko, kailangan kong mag travel abroad. Ang laking kita ang nawala sa akin dahil sa travel ban.

Kaya sinasabi ko ako din ay biktima ng Martial Law, at hindi ko susuportahan kailanman ang anak ng diktador.

Isa pa. Pinadalan mo ako ng video ni Leni kung saan sya ay nagsasabi hindi sya tatakbo. Ang gusto nyong pakita ay si Leni ay nagsisinungaling. Iba yung sinungalin sa nagpalit ng isip. Lahat tayo ay meron karapatan magpalit ng isip.

Lahat tayo ay magpapalit ng isip. E kung si Du30 na idolo mo, palit ng palit ng isip. Sigurado pati ikaw. Ilan beses ka nagpagpalit ng isip mo sa buhay mo? Sinungaling ka ba dahil doon?

Mababaw ang isip ng gumawa ng video na yun. Naniwala ka?

(REE, October 2021)

....

21

World War II / Bataan & Corregidor –

On the recent occasion of the Araw Ng Kagitingan celebratons, I am reposting an article I wrote a few years ago about my father and his role in WW II. I do so in the hope that the younger generations of Filipinos will recount the untold stories of their fathers and grandfathers who heroically served in WW II. Most of the written history of the War in the Philippines has been written from the American perspective, which has reduced the role of the Filipino soldier to a secondary one at best. This must be corrected! –

Dr. Rafael L Evangelista And The 21st Infantry Division, A Story of Heroism, World War II –

My father, Capt. Rafael L Evangelista (Lolo Apeng to our family) was with the 21st Infantry Division that played a key role in the defense of the Abucay, Bataan. He was doctor assigned to the Medical Corps of the USAFFE. After Abucay, he was assigned to the General Field Hospital (No 1?) in Mariveles, Bataan.

My father always had a fascination with native herbal medicine and edible plants. This served him in good stead in the latter part of the defense of Bataan. The Allies, by that time, were running short of both food and medicine. My father took it upon himself to scrounge the mountainsides of Bataan, trudging through the jungles in by himself, sometimes behind enemy lines, to look for both herbal medicine and edible plants for his patients at the General Field Hospital. This was done obviously at great risk to himself.

Shortly before the Fall of Bataan, he and some other Filipino officers of the Medical Corps received official orders from Gen Douglas MacArthur to transfer, as non combatants, to the Malinta Tunnel Hospital in Corregidor. He and his fellow doctors were to be picked up by a US naval PT boat at Mariveles and transferred to Corregidor.The navy boat assigned to take him and his medical team from Mariveles to Corregidor was however commandeered at gun point by American enlisted men who were seeking to escape themselves. My father and his fellow Filipino officers were off loaded by the Americans at gun point before the Filipino doctors could take off. Lolo Apeng and his fellow doctors were able later to find wooden bancas to take them to Corregidor.

My father referred to that particular group of American soldiers who took the boat assigned to his team at gun point as the "biggest bunch of cowards" he ever met in the War. My father and fellow doctors, all Filipinos, were all commissioned officers in the United States Armed Forces in the Far East (USAFFE). The Americans who ordered my father and his companions off the boat were enlisted men led by a sergeant. The Filipinos clearly outranked the Americans. As the boat pulled away, the sergeant tossed his 45 cal pistol to the Filipinos and mockingly told my father and his fellow doctors, who were all unarmed, to defend themselves with the pistol.

Of course, as doctors, they were technically non combatants. As such, they were not allowed to bear arms under the Geneva Convention. To be caught with a firearm, a doctor could be executed on the spot by the enemy. That is why when my father used to scavenge for medical herbs and food behind enemy lines in the mountains of Bataan, he had to travel without firearms.

Lolo Apeng was eventually captured in Corregidor. He was transferred to the prison camps of Capas, Tarlac, and then the Old Bilibid Prison in Manila. After he was released from there, he traveled to Baguio, where he surreptitiously resumed his medical services for American strugglers and Filipino Guerrillas in the Mountain Province and neighboring provinces.

To get to these provinces, Lolo Apeng travelled through the mountain passes of the town of Malico between the Mountain Province and Nueva Ecija mostly in the dead of night. He would leave our residence in Baguio City sometimes three or four times a month, fetched by mysterious men at night. These men turned out to be guerrillas in the Resistance. More often than not, he would be led by the guerrillas towards the town of Malico. It is notable that Malico was used for passage by both the Resistance and the Japanese troops seeking passage to other provinces. Each of those treks of Lolo Apeng were obviously extremely dangerous.

Eventually, Lolo Apeng was captured, imprisoned and severely tortured by the Japanese Kempetai for these activities. The person who turned in my father was our Japanese gardener who had been in the employ of my family for 15 years before the outbreak of WW II. This gardener showed at my parents' house, heading the Japanese arresting party. He was dressed in a full colonel's uniform of the Japanese Army. He was obviously a fifth columnist sent by Japan to the Philippines long before the War.

One of my earliest recollections of Lolo Apeng was when my mother took me to visit him in the Baguio Japanese Kempetai jail. When I saw him, he was hanging by his thumbs with his arms pulled behind his torso and above his head from the prison rafters. His toes barely touched the ground, and he had been beaten to unconsciousness. Nevertheless, Lolo Apeng was released after about two months of severe torture. His Japanese captors could not get him to confess to his guerrilla activities. He told me years after the war that he was convinced that if he had confessed, he would have been killed in retribution.

However, at one time, shortly he was released from that Kempetai jail in Baguio, Lolo Apeng and his family, which included me, were lined up by the Japanese in front of a machine gun and threatened with death if he didn't confess. He did not. Miraculously, we were all released unharmed.

Lolo Apeng survived the imprisonment, the torture and the War. For his efforts, he was awarded after the War the US Prisoner of War Medal by the US Ambassador to the Philippines at the US Embassy in Manila. Long after the award of the Prisoner of War Medal, Lolo Apeng also received the US Congressional Gold Medal (along with some his fellow Veterans who served with the USAFFE in WW II).

This however was sparse recognition from the US for Filipinos who fought and died for the cause of freedom in a War not of their making, and who received nothing in return from their colonial master, the United States.

One thing is noteworthy about my father and his Filipino comrades in arms. Although they were all Filipinos, they served while the Philippines was a colony of the United States. During this colonial period, Filipinos were arguably American nationals. Filipino citizens as such were non existent from a legal perspective at that time. Indeed, Filipinos of that era were issued American passports. It is one of the tragedies of Philippine-American relations however that Filipino veterans of the USAFFE in WW II were not granted the same benefits and recognition as Americans who had served in the same theater of the War. It is an injustice still waiting to be addressed and corrected even as the last Filipino USAFFE veterans have passed on.

Lolo Apeng was technically assigned to the 21st Infantry Division, USAFFE, at the time of the onslaught of the Japanese in 1942 in Bataan. And he and the 21st Infantry Division were assigned to an area of Bataan where some of the fiercest battles of the War took place.The 21st Infantry Regiment, 21st Infantry Division (Philippine Army, Reserve), along with 41st Div and 51st Div Regiments (all Philippine Army, Reserve) together with a lone regular US Army unit, the 57th PS comprised of Filipino enlisted men with American NCOs and officers, held the Abucay Line on the eastern side of the

Bataan peninsula (II Corps AOR) from January 9-23, 1942.

This major action happened after the Battle of Layac Junction, which was the first delaying action against the Japanese attempt to penetrate the Bataan Peninsula. The maps available depict the action in Layac Junction and the Abucay Line. It is interesting to note that the so-called poorly-trained, newly-mobilized USAFFE Divisions, with the exception of the lone all-American infantry unit, the 31st Regiment, and the 26th & 57th PS Regiments, were committed as the vanguard to check the Japanese initial advance into Bataan.

However, the truth is, those were all the fighting units the USAFFE had. The other USAFFE Divisions, regular and reserve, were on the western side of Bataan. The other remaining all-American fighting units that were held in reserve were the 4th Marine Regiment, which was initially held in Corregidor as beach defense (some were also held south in the Bataan rear CP and Mariveles as base security), and the provisional infantry battalions comprised of former US Army Air Corps and Naval units (without planes and ships).

Regardless, history points out that despite the fact the Abucay Line was eventually abandoned, the Japanese suffered heavy casualties, making them re-think their way forward. Except for Japanese attempts to flank I Corps AOR via landings on the west coast of Bataan (which failed), the Battles of the Pockets and the Points (where the Japanese also suffered tactical defeats), no successful major action was made by the Japanese until their main and final offensive beginning April 1942.

By April 1942, the Filipino-American defenders were exhausted, starved and diseased, their numbers reduced by massive casualties. In the final analysis, the Filipino-American defenders lost a logistics battle, and not because they were tactically inferior or less courageous than the Japanese. Despite what others have noted as inadequacies in equipment, armament, food and medicine, there is little doubt that they would have fought to the bitter end had they had the means to do so.

My father, Lolo Apeng, marched and fought with heroes, the Filipinos who served in the USAFFE. As fate would have it, these Filipino hero veterans were subjected to the insidious provisions of the infamous US Recission Act of 1946, the law that deprived all USAFFE Filipinos of recognition and honor for their heroism in WW II.

I repost this story of my father in the hope that the families of the Filipino soldiers who fought so heroically during WW II will come forward and write about their ancestors. There is still so much left untold about the heroism of the Filipino soldier in World War II.

Rafael E Evangelista, Former National Commander of Bataan & Corregidor, And proud son of WW II Hero and Veteran, Dr. Rafael L Evangelista USAFFE

(Updated, 13 March 2022)

....

22
THANK YOU, LORD

Thank you, Lord, for these "little things":

-the rays of hope a smile can bring,
-the clasp of a loving, helping hand,
-the soothing comfort of "I understand,"
-the warmth of the sun after the rain,
-the calming comfort after the pain,
-friends that stay midst trials and tears,
-the peace GOD gives to calm our fears,
-for all His mercy and His love,

-and prayers answered from above!

Raffy Evangelista, Oct 13, 2022

....

23
The Value Of The Gift

It is the value of things that counts, not the price. There is a big difference between value and price. As we hurry along to catch special day deadlines and buy gifts for the many on our gift lists, let us reflect on how many of the gifts we intend to give out are motivated by love or friendship. The kiss of a loved one has more value than a pricey gift given without love.

And the most valuable love gift we will ever receive is Jesus. It is for this reason that we can't, we shouldn't, take Christ out of our gift giving, because Jesus is the ultimate gift. He came to sacrifice His life for us to save us. His was the supreme sacrifice of love, His invaluable gift of life to us in exchange for His own on the Cross.

May our Lord Jesus be with you everyday of the rest of your life. God bless you always.

(Raffy Evangelista, 11 December 2022)

....

24
Love's Sunlight

Wake me up inside,
I feel the stirrings outside.
I know the gifts the mornings sing
And all the joy that they can bring.

But inside me night shadows
Still pace as rainbows prance
Outside in colors of the sun,
Awake before the night is done.

Where are the shining stars,
To tell me where you are?
In the darkness of my room
I search the shifting gloom.

Then I feel fingers of the sun
Warming the cold, fled and gone.
I blink to make the waking slow
And feel warmth just softly grow.

Love's light is what makes life
Worth struggling through strife,
Worth living through darkness.
Love blots out the sadness.

I shall win love's sunlight
By fighting for what is right
Beyond the distant gate,
Never for what I hate.

(Raf Evangelista, 24 May 2023)

....

25
Again and Again

If there is a single light
At the close of the singing
On our long path of life,
I Shall be by you, darling.

I will look for you among
The tulips that grow free
Among the everglades.
I will be there besides thee.

Together we shall romp
Towards the bridge of life,
That crosses to the skies,
Through happiness or strife.

Keep your light to guide me
So I can meet you there.
I will follow your light.
It Does not matter where.

Yours has been the hand
To hold me, yours has been
the heart to embrace me,
You, a miracle that I have seen.

When the sky meets land
When the clouds meet the rain,
I will be there besides you,
Loving you again and again.

(REE, 11 November 2022)

....

26
FLY, FLY, FLY

You hover over us in love,
Even as you had done ...
The sparkle of light above,
Just below the rising sun,

Is that you with angel wings
Amongst the clouds? You ...
Smiling, laughing, seeing,
With the sparkle of dew?
I see on your radiant face
The brillance of the sun
Reflecting Heaven's grace
On a beloved, favored one!
You have crossed over
From dark side to the light
Eyes open, seeing, blessing!
No darkness blocking sight,
No fears tearing from without,
No tears to wonder about.
Only the gentle gaze looking,
Caring, loving from within.
You never ever whined
You never complained.
Only smiles that shined,
Though great the pain.
Fly, my friend, fly from here
Free of pain, free of fear.
You are whole, you are free.
God's love hearken unto thee!

Fly, good, blessed one!
Fly! Fly!

(Rafael E Evangelista, 2 February 2021)

....

27
The Sun God

The chatter of the birds
fall silent with the

growing stillness of the
symphony of deepening night.
The busy white clouds
that danced to the blaze of morning,
retreat silently at evening
to the home of the golden sun,
now dressed with in the
colours of his cloak:
an abstraction of rainbow strokes.
and as evening comes,
the sun god, knowing
that he soon must go,
tears up his robe of prismatic colours,
and spreads it across the
western clouds in benediction,
a fond farewell and a promise
of his return on the morrow.
His colours flame and blaze,
reflections on the sea,
whose rouge - lipped waves
lap gently, heaving ruby swells,
slowly, kaleidoscopically,
rocking the night to a tantalizing
deep and profound sleep.
I slowly turn away from the
framed abstraction in my window
of fading colors of purple
blue orange and crimson.
Reassured by his promise
that he will return in the morrow
in a blaze of gold and silver,
I slide into the gentle embrace
of night and the caressing breeze,
and fall Into peaceful slumber.

(Raf Evangelista, 13 March 2023)

....

28
Opening Remarks –

The Barangay and How It Relates to Mater et Magistra (the encyclical on Church/Christianity and Social Progress - St Pope John Paul XXIII)

Over the years, we have been faced with "the erosion of the anthropological foundations which ground the possibility of civil society." What we are facing is "a situation where the indispensable bases for an authentically democratic and Christian society have been radically undermined.

What are the anthropological foundations of civil society? Basically they are four: truth, justice, peace, love. These foundations have been violently shaken. Thus,

1) In the conduct of public affairs truth has been badly battered. People have learned to believe as true the exact opposite of what is officially announced. And when the untruth is made public it is hypocritically given the semblance of an honorable disguise.

2) Justice has been brutalized beyond recognition. The lady of justice has been stripped of her blindfold and the balance scales are often replaced by the truncheon or by the barrel of a gun.

3)The meaning of peace has been distorted. Peace has come to mean the desolation of a hamletted village or the grim visage of a silenced salvage victim.

4) Love at best has come to manifest itself in the shape of wasteful display and at worst in human sacrifice at the altar of national security.

And it is in this critical context that we, the people, are challenged to make a contribution. We have been, by God's grace, provided with a vehicle to achieve and reinstall the four foundations of civil society in our country. That vehicle is the barangay. Today, let us ask ourselves. What is it that we as Filipinos can offer to our communities and our country to achieve the social progress espoused by Pope John Paul XX III?

One answer we can offer our people is "the barangay," and all it explicitly and implicitly implies!

But "what, why, how" the barangay is for us to learn about and to implement in each of our communities.

We have much still to learn and understand!
(Raf Evangelista, 2022)

....

29
A Love Poem
(for Tatty Bear, our fur baby)

From Mama:
Dear Tatty:
One More Time

You embraced my love for you
When time took you from me.
Then you took my soul away too
When you left to cross the sea.
I looked to God's heaven
And tried to see you there.
I felt your touch just then
As perfumed love filled the air.
When your paws embraced me,
It was just for one more time.
I do not think anyone could see,
but you were really there for me.
We will meet again one day,

But for now I can really say
You came and cared
And once more shared
your deep love for me!
Till then farewell,
dear Tatty. Mama

(Raf Evangelista, 24 March 2023)

....

30
From your furry son, Bear:

Grieve Not, Papa
You grieve for me
Because I left your side.
Can you not clearly see
My love for you abides?
My love shall forever be,
And I know that you love me.
Your grief will go one day,
But my love for you will stay.
As much as my love for you,
So did you love me too.
Wipe tears from your eyes,
True love never ever dies.
Our goodbyes are not forever.
Someday we shall be together,
And under God's skies of blue,
I will still be in love with you. Papa,
I love you! I truly do! Bear

(Your beagle PWD, pet with disability, furry son)

(Bear passed about a year ago. One year after, or just a few days ago, his golden retriever sister, Chelsea, also travelled to the rainbow bridge)

Raf Evangelista 19 March 2023

....

31
To Bear and Chelsea, My Two Fur Siblings Who Have Gone On To Rainbow Heaven:

Brother Bear, Sister Chelsea,
what are you two doing up there?
Do you own the piece of heaven
that you now share?

Sometimes when I look
up to the sky, I think
I can see your faces
among the clouds that fly.

You both seem to be very
happy where you are,
Playing among the golden
sun and silver stars.

Please say hello to God for me,
and greet the angels too. Tell them that
I have been well behaved
since I was last with you.

There are nights that
I wake up looking for your touch,
Wondering where you are,
and missing you so very, very much.

*Thank you for being an
older brother and sister to me.
Without your love, I do not know
where I would be.*

*I promise to behave now
that I'm the only one.
I shall try, and keep trying,
to be good till every day is done.*

*Watch over me as you did
when you were here.
I shall look after Mama and Papa,
both of whom we hold so dear.*

*I shall love them both
just as you loved them too.
I shall love them because they
were soulmates to the both of you.*

*Fly high, to God's high heavens.
Fly, my siblings, Fly!
On your angel wings,
soar on to God's blue sky!*

*Fly! Your youngest sister,
Cider PS: Mama and Papa
asked me to tell you that they love you,
and that they miss you too.*

(Bear, our eldest beagle, and Chelsea, our golden retriever, passed on roughly a year apart from each other in 2022 and 2023. Cider, also a beagle, is the youngest and last remaining of our 3 fur babies. - REE)

(Raf Evangelista, 25 March 2023)

....

32
At The Shaking

Pay attention to God whisper,
So you don't have to listen
When the shouting starts.
Slow down during vespers
No need to run and hasten,
Say prayers from the heart.
Often, the whisper you hear
Is God's grace talking to you.
If shaking begins, do not fear,
God's faithfulness will be true,
And His love will hold you near.
And when the battle is sounded,
Hold on, have faith, be grounded.
Never let go of His loving Hand.
But prepare to make your stand.

(Raf Evangelista, 27 March 2023)

....

33

Maybe, Again, Finally

A poem failed national elections-
Maybe, Again, Finally

*Maybe the tip of starlight
was truly there.*

*Maybe it was not a
mirage I saw, despite the
darkness of the seas caused
by thirty one million ghosts.*

*Maybe the tip of the brightness –
the gathering of fifteen million
stars has been awakened.*

*Maybe this tip will prove to be
a shining beacon for those
still hidden in the dark beyond.*

*Maybe I can follow this tip of light,
and find my hope again,
find my courage again,
and navigate and find my way
through the frothing and
seething waters*

To calmer seas somewhere.

Today,

I will follow that light!

Then …

Maybe,

Tomorrow!

Someday!

One day!

And then,

Again,

Finally!
(REE, 4 July 2022)

....

34
Summer Solstice

We search for cooling shadows
Amongst the leafless trees,
Brown with blazing sunshine
And the hot summer breeze.

All shade has danced away
Under the stern glare of the sun.
The sweet songs of springtime
Receded, and now are gone.

The waves of migratory birds
That used to circle the skies
With color, chirping and dance,
Have flown on without goodbyes.

We miss the soft muted whispers
Of the evening grassy lands,
And, under star filled skies, the
Gentle waves on ocean sands.

Pray, let us stay with each other
Until flowers bloom once more,
And soothing showers again return
To calm distant restive shores.

There are none to lead but us
Through this hot, sweltering land.
When morning comes to midnight,
I will need your guiding hand.

When the sun begins to set
And the moon rules the skies
I will seek love's cooling breath
And the sweetness of your sighs.

Come walk with me, my darling,
As we hold our hands together.
Let flowers of love bloom again
Past the scorching heat of summer.

(Rafael E Evangelista, 13 May 2021)

....

35
Among Spring Rainbows

Sharing love poems for all who have lost loved ones recently or in the past:
Among Spring Rainbows

A breeze blows through my window.
In the shifting light of the evening star,
The silk curtains sigh and gently flow,
A song of love singing but from afar.

Is that you, my love, in the gentle light
Of the evening sky singing softly to me?
I reach out to catch and touch the sight
Of the star's soft rays I can clearly see.

A night bird coos in the deep shadows

Of needle pines and late winter green,
Coaxing spring blooms to show and grow,
For now in darkness they sleep unseen.

The sky and the woods speak of love
Even as I miss you dearly through the night.
I will search for you among stars above,
And will love you with the coming light.

Wait for me wherever you might be
I will be searching for you in the spring
Beyond the mountains and the sea
To hear the music of your love sing.

I know that you have waited for me
Through all these winter days gone,
Your smile once more I hope to see
Beneath spring rainbows of the sun.

(Raffy Evangelista 18 April 2021)

....

36
A Smile In Your Heart

One day I will go on a journey,
To where love always abides.
I shall love you still so dearly,
And forever be at your side.

Even when heaven calls me home,
My vows to you will not be broken.
I promise you I shall never roam,
Even while I journey on to heaven.

I mean to forever share your heart,

And always have you be a part of me,
For God never meant us to be apart,
But for us to be united for all eternity.

Then when heaven becomes my home,
I will wait, and neither grieve or mourn,
For I know that one day you will join me
With the coming of that blessed morn.

I will wait for that blessed day
When we two shall again be one
And you and I can always stay
United under God's Forever Sun.

And when I pass, look after me,
Even if we are physically apart,
Look to where I shall always be,
A smile in the corner of your heart.

(Raffy Evangelista, 15 March 2021)

....

37
FLY, My Friend, FLY

You hover over us in love,
Even as you had done ...
The sparkle of light above,
Just below the rising sun,
Is that you with angel wings
Amongst the clouds? You ...
Smiling, laughing, seeing,
With the sparkle of dew?
There! On your radiant face
The brillance of the sun
Reflecting Heaven's grace

On a beloved, favored son?
You have crossed over
From the dark to light.
Blue skies, no cloud cover,
No darkness blocking sight.
No more fears tearing
At the body's pulsating skin.
But the gentle gaze looking,
Caring, loving from within.
You never ever whined
You never complained.
Only smiles that shined
From God's Love again.
Fly, Friend, fly from here
Free of pain, free of fear.
You are whole, you are free.
God's love hearken unto thee!
Fly! Fly! Fly!

(Rafael E Evangelista, 19 April 2021)

....

38
My Song Is For You

I dedicate this poem to all those who have lived a full God filled life:
My Song Is For You,

Lord I have the words.
When will the music come?
I want to sing my song
Before the setting sun.

Come strum the music,
Lord, So I can put my words

to song Of praise, and
love, and joy; I have waited for so long.

Oh Lord, I hear distant strains,
A beautiful melody I hear.
It is the music of the wind
Whispering gently in my ear.

Help me sing my song, O Lord,
The words I have within me.
By Your grace, the wind is singing
My song that's meant to be.

Words I started writing
Since I was a little boy,
Oh Lord, hear my song
Of praise, of love and joy.

Now as the sun begins to fade,
And I am growing old,
And the wind begins its song,
My story will be told.

You have strummed the music.
Please put my words to song.
The song, my Lord, is for You.
I have waited for so long.

(Rafael E Evangelista, 18 July 2020)

....

39
The Echo Of The Spoken Word

How the spoken word echoes and resonates depends not only on what, but also when and where the words are spoken. In an empty chamber, words mean nothing, say nothing, and come to nothing. It is different when a message of love, giving and forgiving comes from the chambers of the heart, and is addressed, heart to heart, to one in need of compassion, respect and understanding. The word so spoken reverberates, resonates and touches with an indelible imprint on the soul which listens to the echoes that have come from the heart.

Raf Evangelista 7 May 2023

....

40
THE SACRIFICE OF LOVE
(A Poem Honoring Filipino US Congressional Gold Medal Awardees and Other Veterans)

We salute our vets,
We salute our flag,
As we now remember ...
For love, some sacrificed some...
And others sacrificed all!

Prayers from our hearts,
Blossoms on the ground,
White crosses that remind ...
Many sacrificed some...
And many sacrificed all!

Our country 'tis to thee,
Our land of liberty,
That to our fathers gave ...
Some sacrificing some...
Some sacrificing all!

We now stand proud and tall
By warmth of freedom blessed,
Because they marched before...
In pitched battle risking some...
In throes of death giving all!

If today, the air around is free
And the skies above are clear,
Remember there were those...
Who for love gave some...
While others gave their all!

Straighten wayward crosses,
Plant flowers on their graves,
Say a prayer for them who were
Wounded, died... or forgotten...
Who gave some... or maybe all!

Do not let their pictures fade,
In our hearts, or minds, or homes.
Tell the children of the heroes...
Who risked their lives for them...
Sacrificing blood... or life for all!

(Rafael E. Evangelista, December 29, 2019) by

The US Congressional Gold Medal is the highest civilian award of the United States. The US Congress approved the award of this medal to the Filipino soldiers who served in the United States Armed Forces of the Far East (USSAFE), the Philippine Scouts, USAPIP, and recognized guerrilla groups during WW II.

On December 29, 2019, fifty + Filipino veterans received the US CGM, the third group of Filipino veterans to do so. The late father of Rafael E. Evangelista, Dr. Rafael L. Evangelista, was one of the awardees. Dr. Evangelista was a member of the Medical

Corps of the USAFFE. He served in Bataan and Corregidor, was tortured by the Japanese for Guerrilla activities, but survived the War.

It is in honor of all Filipino WW II veterans that Raffy Evangelista has written this poem.

....

41
Broken Crayons

A throbbing heart is a fragile heart
That can be filled with bitterness Or joy.
The choice is often yours.
You can chose to mend and start,
And fill your lives with loveliness
By painting a different course.

There are hiccups along the way –
Pain, anger, and stumbling blocks.
Paint only smiles of the early sun.
Hold on to its bright golden rays,
And banish those painful shocks
Along blighted paths you've run.

Broken crayons can paint the sky
In colors - red, blue and green,
There is much that a heart can do:
Forget hurt, paint sunshine, or try.
Light in shade that flits unseen,
Can be painted as rainbows too.

Colors change the world we live in.
Let us look beyond the bend.
Let us paint roses and clover,
Not shadows of what has been.
Keep painting. Darkness will end,
If you spread the light all over.

Hold hands, and never let go.
Your broken crayons and mine
Can still paint rainbows just like so,
And make this world of ours shine…
Paint, dear friend, paint! Go on!
Paint the sun with broken crayons!

Raffy Evangelista 12 June 2022

....

42
The First And Last Times

Two things
I will never forget:
The way you looked
At me the first time,
And the way you looked
At me the last time.

I always watched…
I always watched
And then only acted.
I always watched
With a still heart
And mind… And
I thought I had learned.

When I thought I had
Watched enough,
And learned enough,
I felt I could act upon
The knowledge
I had gained. But sadly,

It turns out that I could not.

When I reached out
To touch you,
You were gone.
I did not act upon
The knowledge gained.
I saw you for a moment.
I saw the way you looked
At me the first time.
But then I missed the
Way you looked at me

The last time.
Then you were gone!
Sadly, I looked away
The time you looked
At me for the last time.
And when I looked back
You were gone
For the very Last time.
The last time that
Broke my heart!
(Raffy Evangelista, 29 April 2023)

....

43
Power of Kindness:

There are many virtues: Piety, Faith, Humility; Honesty, Chastity, Perseverance but the King of Virtues is Kindness, Kindness to others.

It is an active virtue: you have to act upon it; it is also a double blessing: it blesses the one who receives and the one who gives the act of Kindness. It causes many ripples in the pool of life; and Kindness gives lasting memories because although you may no longer remember, people will remind you of the Kindness you gave.

What then is Kindness:

1. "Kindness is more important than wisdom, and the recognition of this is the beginning of wisdom." - Theodore Isaac Rubin

2. "Kindness is the language which the deaf can hear and the blind can see." -Mark Twain

3. "You cannot do a kindness too soon, for you never know how soon it will be too late." -Ralph Waldo Emerson

4. "Constant kindness can accomplish much. As the sun makes ice melt, kindness causes misunderstanding, mistrust, and hostility to evaporate." - Albert Schweitzer

5. Love and kindness are never wasted. They always make a difference. They bless the one who receives them, and they bless you, the giver."-Barbara de Angelis

6. "Remember there's no such thing as a small act of kindness. Every act creates a ripple with no logical end." -Scott Adams

7. "The level of our success is limited only by our imagination and no act of kindness, however small, is ever wasted." -Aesop

8.Be kind! Be kind to others! Give without counting the cost, or fight without heeding the wounds, to toil and not to seek for rest, save that of knowing that kindness is God's Will. -Ignatius of Loyola, paraphrased.

Be kind and you will be an inheritor of God's Kingdom.

Raffy Evangelista 2020

....

44

The Golden Buddah

A treasure hunter named Roger Roxas found this statue in a tunnel network under/near the Baguio General Hospital. This, according to his son, Henry, who was with him at the time. Henry has a picture of the same statue, with the head detached, showing the body cavity full of what appear to be an assortment precious stones. Henry says the statue itself was of pure gold.

Henry says that his father was killed by a single shot to the back of his head under mysterious circumstances after the statue and its contents were confiscated. This confiscation happened during the martial law regime of Ferdinand E Marcos.

According to Henry, a gold plated statute with a non-detachable head was later substituted for the original one. The original, and the contents of precious stones have never been recovered by the Roxas family.

I have seen on social media over the past two or three years, a picture ostensibly of Imelda Marcos viewing what appears to be the same golden buddah that Henry and Roger Roxas were pictured with. It is anyone's guess whether this more recent picture is authentic or not.

Maybe one day, under circumstances that are favaorable, the truth of the Golden Buddah can finally be ferretted out.

(Raf Evangelista, 28 May 2023)

....

45
Holes Fit for Roses

Flowers are usually used to represent love. The heart in this poem, despite the hurts, symbolized by the holes, continues to love, and each hole is filled with a rose (REE)

Holes Fit for Roses

My heart is imperfect,
Full of holes and hurting,
Stretching out to others
In deep hopes of loving.

No two holes the same,
A heart filled with light,
And only pure roses
That fit each hole right.

Relationships I built
Form the fabric of life,
But distance in any form
Cuts sharp like a knife.

To love is to know,
To know is to hold.
I will cherish those loved
Till I have grown old.

It wasn't really my dream,
But it is still fine with me
To have a heart full of holes,
Filled with roses I see.

(Raf Evangelista 23 September 2021)

....

46
The New Suzeraintly

I wrote this in April 2021. It may still be relevant today, with some amendments) –
The New Suzerainty

Suzerainty is a relationship in which one state or other polity controls the foreign policy and relations of a tributary state, while allowing the tributary state to have internal autonomy. The dominant state is called the "suzerain." Suzerainty differs from sovereignty in that the tributary state is technically independent, but enjoys only limited self-rule.

Although the situation has existed in a number of historical empires, it is considered difficult to reconcile with 20th- or 21st-century concepts of international law, in which sovereignty is a binary which either exists or does not. While a sovereign state can agree by treaty to become a protectorate of a stronger power, modern international law does not recognise any way of making this relationship compulsory on the weaker power. Suzerainty is a practical, de facto situation, rather than a legal, de jure one. (Wikipedia)

This is what could happening in our part of the world. China is trying to establish a suzerainty in the Asia Pacifc Region. The obvious intention is for China to be, in the very least, the suzerain or the dominant state in this part of the world. It is trying to exercise control over the foreign policy of the Philippines to the extent of trespassing on Philippines seas, claiming those seas and islands within those seas are China's, and demanding that sea and air passage over the area by other States requires China's permission.

Most Filipinos view the United States as an ally today, even as there seems to be an attempt by some Philippine authorities to create and/or accept a new geopolitical normal of special relations with Mainland China. China is, I believe, trying to replicate on a grander scale the Japanese plan of a greater Asia under the

Japanese Co-Prosperity Sphere. The Philippines had the courage to fight Japan's Imperialism sacrificing over a million Filipino lives to do so. All that sacrifice of lives may go for naught. Sadly, former President Duterte seemed to welcome this attempt by China to establish a new suzerainty. To my mind, the Duterte Government was complicit in this attempt. The present Marcos government is opague on where it stands with China. It seems that Marcos is engaged in the "roll of the dice" game, reaching out in appeasment of our giant neighbor from the north, while playing footsies the our erstwhile ally, the United States.

It was the height of political naïveté for Duterte's Philippines to expect that under China's suzerainty, our country would enjoy the kind of political autonomy that we enjoy today. All that one has to do is to look to the political experience of HongKong and Taiwan with China. China does not endorse real political autonomy, and can and will use draconian measures to retain and increase political, economic, and if need be, military control over a vassal state or territory.

That being the case, do we have to make a choice, as we did at the start of WW II, between two world powers, China or the United States?

(Rafael E Evangelista updated 15 April 2023)

....

47
When A Gold Butterfly Is Born

Just when the caterpillar thinks
That its ugly, its hard life is over.
It turns into a butterfly.
And then It spreads its wings and flies.
This is us and the life we face.

Without rain, nothing grows.
Embrace the storms of our lives.
Change, metamorphose, and fly!

Why does beauty seem to
Miss a beat with us,
While others are so fair?
Why are others smarter? Or
Wealthier or more powerful?
Sometimes we wonder
Who or what we are;
Sometimes we ask where
Or how do we fit in.

That is our caterpillar
Wandering in and out
Of our puny lives. Sometimes,
The storms force us to our
Hands and knees.
Then one
Day in God's time, we will
Soar.
We will fly as butterflies
That have emerged from
Shells in the struggle of life.

God makes us all beautiful
In His own time.
He just uses different colors to paint us.
After the winds and storms,
The rainbows will glisten.
Then it is not the outer shell of
The caterpillar that counts,
But the hidden butterfly
That will surface and fly.

Life goes on, no matter what.
We may change, and our shells

Will even pass away.
But there Is something infinite in all …
We metamorphose in time
In beauty and in splendor Into
God's gold butterflies,
And fly forever more.

(Raffy Evangelista, 28 August 2022)

....

48
Poems:

Sheep?

A nation of sheep
Without a good shepherd
Will be beset upon
By packs of wolves.

(REE, 25 November 2005)

Secrets

Your actions
Will utimately
Give away
The secrets of Your heart.

(REE, 27 November 2005)

Sharing

If there is something better
Than sharing with others
The best of what you have,

It is sharing with others
The best of what you are.

(REE, 14 December 2005)

I Dream Of Spring

The howling September produces
Foaming dark, forboding canopies.
I dream of the crisp coolness and
Brightness of the coming Spring,
When I can hold your hand,
Once more,
Before the leaves begin to die
In the artic cold of winter,
Or burn in the smoldering
Caldroun of the
July summer.

(REE, 21 December 2005)

....

49
Haiku Selection

Friends

Hand in hand through years,
Sun soaked in the warmth of years,
Amidst wrinkled smiles.

(REE, 19 March 2019)

Cleansing Rain

The old horse plods in

The swirling mud, then canters
To the cleansing rain.

(REE, 20 March 2019)

Letting Go

I can let go of
Power and wealth, but not of
The love now distant.

(REE, 22 April 2019)
The Road

Don't pass up today,
Tomorrow may never come,
The road winds on.

(REE, 28 June 2019)

Listen to the Dark*

Nothing to something...
Listen to the darkness and
Hear the light singing.

(REE, 15 October 2019)

Heaven's Fire

Fire from the heavens,
Deep rumblings before the storm,
The anvil of God.

(REE, 30 November 2019) Soar*

I do not pander
To those who would push and shove.

Soaring, should I care?

(REE, 11 December 2019)

Kiss

Kiss the rains falling
Over scorched, burning mountains.
Trees, what remain, weep.

(REE, 25 December 2019)

Trash

Trash in parks and roads,
Trash amongst our leadership,
Trash in minds and hearts.

(REE, 27 December 2019)

Memories

I will write the hurts
On drifting sands, and etch my
Love on solid rock.

(REE, 4 January 2020)

Burning

The earth is burning.
Is it God's wrath or our own
Stupidity? Both?

(REE, 5 January 2020)

Embers

In the despair of
Darkest winter burns softy
The embers of spring.

(REE, 6 January 2020)

Colored Glasses*

Through the prism of
Colored glasses: softly
Fall. Then, Winter sharply.

(REE, 6 January 2020)

Home*

Going home is just
Beyond the bridge of darkness
To light all over.

(REE, 7 January 2020)

Indifferent*

I, indifferent?
Should I care, if you do not
Make a difference?

(REE, 8 January 2020)

War Rumblings

Flashes in the dark.
Drums of war rumble, but rains
Drench the roaring fires.

(REE, 11 January 2020)

Scorched

The tear slowly falls,
The last of many that fell.
The scorched heart rages.

(REE, 12 January 2020)

White Fire

Once the line is crossed
Where white fire both burns and soothes,
There is no return.

(REE, 29 January 2020)

Love of Self

Why must it be so?
There's a lot of self in you,
Taking, not giving.

(REE, 3 February 2020)

Love's Meaning

Building means giving,
But love simply comes to naught
Without forgiving.

(REE, 4 February 2020)

Unseen Piper

We all march to the
Tune of the unseen piper's
Haunting melody.

(REE, 5 February 2020)

Ate

I reach out my hand
To one I loved all these years,
Borne from the same womb.

(REE, 5 February 2020)

Go low,

Why?
Why must we go low?
We can't go high anymore,
Because others won't?

(REE, 7 February 2020)

We Are More

They win by making

You feel that you are alone ...
There are more of us.

(REE, 9 February 2020)

My World

There is joy that's found
In simplicity of life,
The world I hope for.

(REE, 15 February 2020)

Populism

Not allowed to speak,
Not allowed to criticize,
The freedom bell tolls.

(REE, 29 February 2020)

Once,

Valentine
A kaleidoscope
Of many moments now gone,
A portrait of love.

(REE, 14 March 2020)

Political Winds

Shifting of the winds,
Where will they carry me to,
Peace or turbulence?

(REE, 22 March 2020)

Distant Light

A faint light flickers,
A star or distant firefly.
In the dark, who knows?

(REE, 25 March 2020)

My Dog

Left In the darkness,
I Raised my hand to stroke his head,
But he wasn't there.

(REE, 27 March 2020)

Taho

The vendor searches
Forlornly for the children
Who used buy taho.

(REE, 30 March 2020)

Hungry*

Hunger stalks the land
From dark sea to fearful sea,
Waves from same waters.

(REE, 1 April 2020)

On My Own

I bow my head as
I hear the clap of thunder.
I am on my own.

(REE, 10 April 2020)

Broken Pieces

I held out my hand.
You refused to walk with me...
Broken pieces fell.

(REE, 21 April 2020)

Fly With Me*

Why do you have doubts?
Before the sun disappears,
Fly away with me.

(REE, 29 April 2020)

Silence

The laughter shattered,
A tear ripples on the pond,
Then awkward silence.

(REE, 12 May 2020)

Goodbyes

Why are there goodbyes?
Do things really have to end?
Go then. Say nothing.

(REE, 25 May 2020)

 Life and Death

Defeat death in life.
Do not be pushed by darkness,
Till death takes you home.

(REE, 1 June 2020)

I am heartbroken.
My soul may not remember
You, when I am gone.

The junkyard filled with
Bones of the old forgotten,
Rusting in the wind.

Nothing, nothing stirs,
But a drum throbs faintly,
Beating of a heart.

Sunrise once again
Beyond dark skies and thunder,
The people as one.

Standing on the porch,
Watching you walk away, it
Seems like yesterday.

The morning will come
From where I shall keep searching.
For now the night grows.

The mask clouds my breathe
So that I can hardly breath
The air that we breath!

On the lonely road,
Too far to travel back,
Blackness up ahead.

The rolling heavens
Stirs up golden clouds
With claps of thunder.

*You're so far away..,**
Can you even hear my voice?
You stopped listening.

Shadows race across T*
he grasslands, chasing after
Clouds that paint the sky.

I embrace tonight
To be able to promise
Light for tomorrow.

*It is in the dark**

That I can see the sunshine;
I close my eyes now.

Why are there endings?
Are evers not forevers?
Each second ticked, lost?

I was crestfallen.
I'd never see you again
Smiling through the rain.

Broken pieces of
Today dumped in the dust bins
Of forgotten days.

It is storming outside,
But I do not really care.
I have shut the door.

We Cannot Breathe

Your knee's on our necks,
Ours, not just George Floyd's,
And we cannot breathe.

(REE, 31 May 2020)

I Can't Breathe

Mama,
I can't breathe!
The morning is turning dark.
Now I cannot see.

(REE, 1 June 2020)

I am drained of smiles...
Lost behind the drapes, the sun!

Please bless me with tears.

(REE, 4 June 2020)

Before the day ends,
Let me embrace you once more,
Before darkness comes.

We are connected,
All our minds, hearts and souls are.
Let us take a knee.

I will walk with you
No matter the churning skies.
Your hand lights the way.

Everybody smiles,
Everybody cries, sometimes,
Even through the sun.

Don't just turn away,
I have been waiting so long.
I ask you to stay.

There's a void in me.
It's been fifteen years ago.
It's time to let go.

Rainbows on the Desert Floor

Carpets of flowers
On the arid desert floor,
Rainbows without rain!

(REE, 27 August 2020)

....

50
Manny Valdehuesa

I prepared this tribute to a very good friend, Manuel Valdehuesa, who passed away a short while ago. He and I founded the Gising Barangay Movement with the purpose of establishing true democracy at grassroots level. This tribute is not only a testimony to the Man, but also to his vision. –

A Tribute To A Visionary And A Patriot

Manny Valdehuesa truly believed in the GBM slogan that called for the empowerment of the people at the grassroots. The slogan reads: "Without the direct democracy of the Small Barangay Republic, the legitimacy of our government and political system will always be suspect."

Manny insisted that GBM must be committed to democratic methods even as it works for revolutionary change. Manny constantly urged Filipinos to reform their sovereign role in the governance of their small Barangay republics, all 42,000 plus of them. He urged them to take control of their Barangays, a revolutionary change of political mind set even now.

Reconfigured around these 42,000 + Barangays, Manny's vision was that the Republic's superstructure would assume a pyramidal shape with 3 layers:

1. The primary layer and broad base of our Democracy - these 42,000 + Barangay governments;

2. The intermediate layer - the 1,600 + municipal and provincial governments; and

3. The top layer - the national government located at the pyramid's peak.

The primary layer, or broad base of the political pyramid, Manny always said, is supposed to stabilize the overall government vertical symmetry and balance, if Democracy is to survive.

On the other hand, a government where all power emanates from the national layer is bound to be unstable, standing as it would on the apex of the pyramid. And oftentimes this inverted pyramid translates to dictatorship and autocratic rule.

People empowerment was a vision that Manny shared with President Ramon Magsaysay, who he admired. Magsaysay wrote, "I believe that the government starts at the bottom and moves upward, for government exists basically for the welfare of the masses of the Nation."

Manny's vision is echoed in the 1987 Constitution which states that "Sovereignty resides in the people and all governmental authority emanates from them."

His vision is reflected in the Local Government Code which provides for a parliamentary form of government at the Barangay level, with the Barangay Assembly as the de facto parliament, the highest official political, cultural and social body in the Barangay. And who comprise the Barangay Assembly? All the Barangay residents, the People.

Manny talked about People Empowerment as early as the mid 1960s. He used to visit me in Washington DC where I partnered in the International Law Firm of Baker & McKenzie. Manny's favorite conversation points centered on his "People Empowerment" experiences in Israel's kibutzes and Switzerland's cantons.

However, it was really in mid 1998 that Gising Barangay was born. As Manny himself wrote in an article published by Google, "It was then that a former UN executive from Mindanao and a lawyer banker from Manila actively started toying with the idea of a grass roots movement to promote an assertive brand of citizen sovereignty." That UN executive was, of course, Manny, and the lawyer banker just happened to be me.

But then, it bothered Manny that some consider the 1986 People Power Revolution, and hence by extrapolation the 1987 Constitution, as failures in people empowerment.

Is that so?

Manny and I also had discussions on this issue.

Manny and I believed that EDSA was an unfinished, not a failed, revolution. We believed that there had to be five stages to complete it:

1. The Revolt itself;

2. A new Constitution and implementing laws;

3. Education and involvement of the people in the empowerment process, specially at Barangay level;

4. Election of competent, trustworthy and knowlegeable officials, at Barangay level, who believe in people empowerment; and

5. Establishment of model barangays in various regions of the Philippines.

Of these five stages, only the first two have been accomplished.

Why?

A survey some years ago revealed that the People empowerment provisions of the Constitution and implementing laws are ignored or poorly understood by government officials. And to make things worse, their constituents know little or nothing about them, specially their role in the Barangay's governing process. These are the main reasons why the EDSA Revolution is still unfinished. To this day, few understand what a "Public Servant" truly means.

Reflecting on the GBM slogan that we are committed to, GBM still has its work cut out for it, now more than ever. There is obviously still much to be done to complete our role in the People Power Revolution.

I am sure that Manny, by God's will, is cheering the Filipino on towards the completion of the Revolution, and the vision of grassroot governance that he was such a staunch advocate of.

In closing, let me say that it has been an honor and privilege to have been associated with Manny for the past 56 years.

Manny, I salute you! You belong to the ages!

Raf Evangelista 17 September 2021

....

51
Bayan: SONG TO MY COUNTRY

I have the words within me.
Is the music ready to play?
I must sing your song before
My evening turns to gray.

The wind strums the music,
Now I put the words to song
To proclaim that I salute you.
Bayan, I have waited for so long.

Those distant strains of
The Pambansang Awit I hear.
It is your music in the wind,
Whispering gently in my ear.

People have marched to your song,
Its words stir the heart within me.
The song that the wind is singing,
Is your song that's meant to be.

My Country, 'tis to Thee

Words Pledged, I vividly recall:
Patriotism, loyalty, and courage,
Learned when I was very small.

Now in face of evil, I will be loyal.
And I shall be brave and strong.
Bravery, strength go hand in hand
To defend you against all wrong.

Pilipinas, I nurture you in my heart.
We are what we are because of you.
The struggle for truth is about to start.
Lessons learned must now ring true.

My world must not begin to fade until
I've shared my stories of heroes bold.
The wind is singing their marching song.
Their story of valor will now be told.

The wind sings in soft rhythm of
The source of strength and love.
The song, Bayan, too is about you,
Singing blessings from above.

Bayan ko, sa manlulupig,
Hindi ako pasisiil!

(Rafael E Evangelista, 24 January 2022)

....

52
Road Of Life

We are all pilgrims
On this road called Life.
Some choose the lighted path

For fear of pain or strife.
Others, for the same reason,
Try taking different routes,
And travelling in the dark,
Are lost in the roundabouts.

Others move on to roads
Leading nowhere, left or right,
Blindly, without rhyme or reason,
Without thought or even sight.
Their ways give no guarantee
They will reach the goals they seek.
The winding road of life is difficult
For the sightless and the weak.

Life traversed alone is precipitous.
We all need a loving, guiding hand,
Amidst travails and uncertainties,
To help us make a stand.
No man is an island unto himself,
And no man can survive alone.
Take my hand, I ask of you,
And gently guide me home.

(Raf Evangelista, 29 May 2023)

....

53
Colors

Quite frankly, I do not agree that people should be typed by the color of their skin. To begin with, there is no such thing as a "White" person. Put a white sheet of paper beside any "White" man. He will most certainly not be white. The so called "White" man is pink and all the shades from there to flushed red. So when some, and there are many, talk about people of color" to refer to the brown, black and yellow populations, the little bell of racism in my brain starts ringing.

Wittingly or unwittingly, the phrases "I am White" and you are a "Person of Color" is racism itself at its most insidious. It translates to "I am White! I am special and unique! All other races are colored and belong to the "crass hoipoloi." The expression of "People of Color" has become to some "White" people a pejorative to discriminate against non-whites. But these "White" bigots fail to realize and understand that they too are people of color. They too are non-whites!

Sadly, not being black has fairly recently become an issue for some African Americans who resent that they have been relegated to the tail end of the race color spectrum, and therefore resent all non blacks. As a consequence African Americans are venting their resentment against Asian Americans, who the the blacks feel are the "johnny come latelies in the migratory spectrum."

Will the roll of the dice end here? It is very probable that Asian Americans will themselves start pushing back when they have no where to go. Americans do not realize that Asian Americans, including Fil Ams, were among the first people to migrate to America, long before the white Pilgrims did. So much for staking a color claim.

And at the end of it all, I am left wondering what the color of God is!

(Raffy Evangelista, 28 April 2023)

....

54

The Filipino Soldier of WW II (Written on the occasion of National Heroes Day)

Maybe the best way to educate Americans, about WW II, given the distortions of history and all, is to write about it. Which is what I have been trying to do, writing primarily about my father's war exploits. Dad is, in my opinion, one of the most under recognized heroes of WW II, and the only thing he has to show for it from America is the US Prisoner of War medal.

(Since I wrote this piece, my dad has received the US Congressional Gold Medal, as well as a few service medals).

One of the things I would really like to know is how many lives did Dad save, from Hospital No 1 in Mariveles to the hospital in Malinta Tunnel, to the actual battle fronts where he had to expose himself, without arms, in order to save sticken soldiers. How many soldiers and guerrillas, Filipino and American alike, did he save making those dangerous treks through the mountains of the Philippine north, in the middle of the night during the Japanese occupation, for which he was beaten and tortured, and almost killed?

Yet Dad was a member of the USAFFE, which some American writers, have disparaged and branded as cowards! And when Filipino heroism was displayed, Americans have oftentimes dropped the "Filipino" from any recognition, and simply refer to the heroism as "American" spawned. The only Filipino group that has collectively gained American recognition is the Philippine Scouts.

But when the Scouts are written about by American writers, there is always the qualifying clause that they were US trained and equipped. Or else, hardly any reference is made to the fact that they are Filipinos. As if the lack of training and equipment of the USAFFE troops, if true, was the fault of Filipinos. We were a colony of the United States at that time, for heaven's sake. If the USAFFE troops were in fact ill trained and equipped, whose fault was it?

Americans, though only some and not all, can be so crass! Filipinos and Americans were brothers in arms through WW II. Let it remain so. The Philippine portion of WW II would probably have taken much longer to resolve, and maybe the War itself lost, without the Filipino soldier!

Let us honor all veterans, Filipino and Americans, who fought for God and Country during WW II!

(Rafael Evengelista, 25 August 2022, National Heroes' Day)

....

55
Failure of Leadership

Duterte has failed to lead. Specifically, he has failed to set a coherent overall direction and ethos. His own slogan, "tapang at malasakit" [courage with sympathy], has manifested itself in reality as a twisted "tapang-tapangan at bahala kayo" [bluster, threats, and you're on your own], manifested by his cursing, blaming and threats. Notoriously, he directed law enforcement to "shoot to kill", in one public appearance, and then later denied that he said it, or meant it, or something. He has actually told the nation on at least two occasions, "bahala kayo"; and on a later made the admission "na inutil ako." It's in the transcripts. Look it up.

He and his government have failed to construct and propose, let alone follow, a deliberate, detailed plan based on research and solid data. Instead, his government stumbles from one reactionary measure to another, ad hoc et ad Infinitum. Government agencies, in their own silos, have created different sets of guidelines that many times contradict each other, and fail to address contingencies.

The people are literally leaderless. And a leaderless nation can be a dangerous place. Anarchy, misdirection, confusion and violence thrive in a leaderless atmosphere. Duterte should resign, and the Sovereign People must step in to fill the void of of Leadership, the leadership that is Constitutionally vested in them, but has been usurped by populist forces!

(REE, 19 September 2020)

....

www.ingramcontent.com/pod-product-compliance
Lightning Source LLC
Chambersburg PA
CBHW051753250726
48659CB00001B/399